India

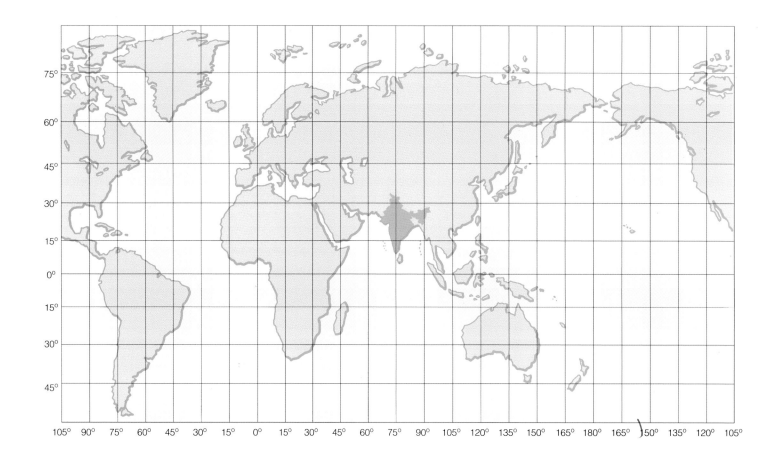

India

Anita Ganeri
Jonardon Ganeri

RAINTREE STECK-VAUGHN
PUBLISHERS

Austin, Texas

Design Roger Kohn
Editor Diana Russell, Helene Resky
DTP editor Helen Swansbourne
Picture research Valerie Mulcahy
Illustration János Márffy
Malcolm Porter
Consultant David Barrs
Commissioning editor Debbie Fox

We are grateful to the following for permission
to reproduce photographs:
Front Cover: Magnum (George Rodger) *above,* Magnum
(Abbas) *below;* The Casement Collection/TRIP, page 18;
Bruce Coleman, page 41 *above* (Dr. M. P. Kahl), 41 *below*
(Gunter Ziesler); Dinodia/TRIP, pages 11 *below,* 13 *above,*
23 *above* (Nadirsh Naoroji), 27 *above,* 32 *above* and *below;*
Eye Ubiquitous/TRIP, pages 10–11, 24 *above* (David
Cumming); Robert Harding Picture Library, pages 8–9
(J. H. C. Wilson), 11 *above* (G. Hellier), 15 (J. H. C. Wilson),
17 *below,* 26–27 (Christopher Rennie), 31 *right,* 33, 35 *below;*
Roger Kohn, pages 13 *below,* 19, 35 *above right;* Magnum,
pages 8 (Raghu Rai), 12 (Steve McCurry), 21 (Abbas),
22 (Bruno Barbey), 24 *below* (Abbas), 25, 27 *below* and
29 *below* (Raghu Rai), 30 (Bruno Barbey), 31 *left* (Raghu Rai),
35 *above left* and 36 *below* (Bruno Barbey), 39 (Gruyaert);
NASA/TRIP, page 42 *below;* Peter Rauter/TRIP, page 29
above; Roger Reynolds/TRIP, pages 37, 40; Helene
Rogers/TRIP, pages 17 *above,* 23 *below,* 39, 43; TRIP,
page 42 *above;* Zefa, pages 14 and 20 (Boutin), 36 *above*
(Cameraman).

The statistics given in this book are the most up-to-date
available at the time of going to press

Printed and bound in Hong Kong by Paramount Printing Group

1 2 3 4 5 6 7 8 9 0 HK 99 98 97 96 95 94

Library of Congress Cataloging-in-Publication Data
Ganeri, Anita, 1961–
India / Anita Ganeri, Jonardon Ganeri.
p. cm. – (Country fact files)
Includes bibliographical references and index.
ISBN 0-8114-2787-0
1. India – Juvenile literature.
I. Ganeri, Jonardon. II. Title. III. Series.
DS407.G323 1995
954–dc20
94-15994
CIP AC

**C
O
N
T
E
N
T
S**

Words that are explained in the glossary are printed in
SMALL CAPITALS the first time they are mentioned in the text.

INTRODUCTION

The world's seventh largest country, India, is a vast land with a huge population. It is also an ancient land with a history reaching back over 5,000 years to the time of the Indus civilization. In about 1500 B.C., this advanced civilization collapsed, and a people called the Aryans invaded northern India from the west. There followed a series of powerful empires and kingdoms until the 8th century A.D. Then Muslims from the Middle East began to establish themselves in India. The first great MOGUL (Muslim) emperor, Babar, came to the throne in 1526. When the Mogul Empire began to crumble in the 18th century, European

▶ *India was once ruled by kings and princes, and some still have their titles and palaces. This picture shows the MAHARAJAH of Varanasi (Benares) in his palace.*

▼ *Many of the slums and shanty-towns in India's cities are home to workers from the countryside.*

INDIA AT A GLANCE

● Area: 1,269,346 square miles (3,287,590 sq km)
● Population (1993): 907,442,000
● Population density: 715 persons per square mile (276 per sq km)
● Capital: New Delhi, population 271,990
● Other main cities: Calcutta 10 million; Bombay 9 million; Delhi 6.7 million; Madras 5 million; Bangalore 3 million
● Highest mountain: Nanda Devi, 25,645 feet (7,818 m)
● Longest river: Brahmaputra, 1,680 miles (2,704 km)
● Languages: Hindi, Sanskrit, English, and 13 other official languages
● Major religions: Hinduism, Islam, Christianity, Sikhism, Buddhism, Jainism
● Life expectancy at birth: 58 years (compared with 75 years in the United States)
● Currency: Rupees, written as Rs
● Economy: Highly dependent on agriculture, but rapidly industrializing
● Major resources: Iron ore, coal, several metals and minerals (especially bauxite and copper ore), gemstones, agricultural land
● Major products: Tea, leather, handicrafts, iron ore, chemicals, cotton goods, jute, silk, engineering goods
● Environmental problems: Air and water pollution from industrial and human waste, deforestation, soil erosion

traders seized their chance to build up their power in the country. The British East India Company gained greater control, and, in 1868, India became part of the British Empire. It was not until 1947 that the country finally gained its full independence.

Because of its great size and its many invaders, India is a land of immense diversity. People in different parts of the country not only look different, they eat different food, wear different clothes, and speak different languages — over 1,500 in total. India is also a place of great contrasts. There are large cities and tiny villages; poverty-stricken slums and fabulously wealthy palaces; penniless beggars and rich film stars. Despite a high level of poverty, India is also among the world's most industrialized countries. It also plays a key role in Asian and international affairs.

This book is an introduction to India. You will find information about the country and its people; the climate and natural resources; how Indian people earn their livings; and about the religions and traditions that play such a large part in their lives.

THE LANDSCAPE

India covers an area of 1,269,346 square miles (3,287,590 sq km) and is shaped roughly like a triangle. From north to south, the country spans about 1,986 miles (3,200 km) and from west to east 1,676 miles (2,700 km). India has land borders with Pakistan, Nepal, China, Afghanistan, Myanmar (Burma), Bhutan, and Bangladesh. It also has over 3,972 miles (6,400 km) of coastline.

India has a varied landscape, ranging from snowcapped mountains in the north to tropical rain forest, palm-fringed beaches, and scorching desert. There are four main geographical regions. The first region consists

KEY FACTS

● At 1,560 miles (2,510 km) the Ganges River is India's second longest river, next to the Brahmaputra. The Hindus regard the Ganges as sacred.
● India is one-third the size of the United States.
● The Himalayas have 95 peaks over 24,650 feet (7,500 m) high. The word *himalaya* means "house of snow."
● The Thar Desert covers about 100,000 square miles (260,000 sq km) — almost twice the size of Bangladesh.

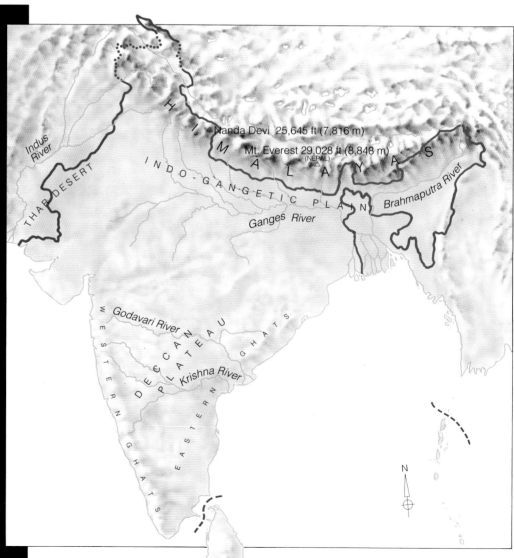

Indus River

THAR DESERT

HIMALAYAS

Nanda Devi 25,645 ft (7,816 m)

Mt. Everest 29,028 ft (8,848 m)
(NEPAL)

INDO-GANGETIC PLAIN

Brahmaputra River

Ganges River

WESTERN GHATS

Godavari River

DECCAN PLATEAU

EASTERN GHATS

Krishna River

N

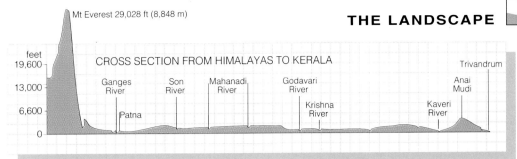

CROSS SECTION FROM HIMALAYAS TO KERALA

Mt Everest 29,028 ft (8,848 m)

feet
19,600
13,000
6,600
0

Ganges River
Patna
Son River
Mahanadi River
Godavari River
Krishna River
Kaveri River
Anai Mudi
Trivandrum

▲ **The ice-capped peaks of the Himalayas are the highest mountains in the world.**

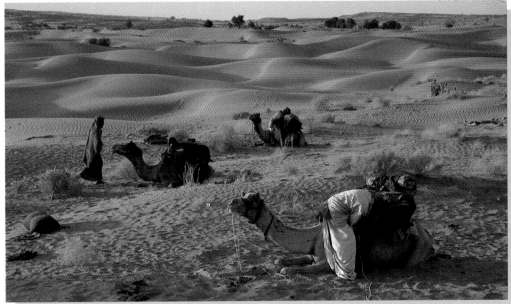

of the mountains that mark India's northern boundary, the Himalayas, which are the world's highest peaks. The Himalayas extend into Pakistan, Nepal, Bhutan, and Tibet. They include the world's highest mountain, Everest, 29,028 feet (8,848 m), on the border between Nepal and Tibet. India's highest mountain, Nanda Devi, 25,645 feet (7,816 m), is also in this mountain range.

The Ganges River flows from the Himalayas across India's second geographical region, the flat Indo-Gangetic Plain, into the ocean at the Bay of Bengal. The plain is a fertile area for growing crops. It is also one of the most densely populated areas of the world. To the south of this plain is the third region, the Deccan Plateau, a large area of raised land. It is bordered by two mountain ranges, the Western and Eastern Ghats. The fourth region is the dry, sandy Thar Desert in Rajasthan in the west.

▲ **The Thar Desert covers much of the western state of Rajasthan. It is hot, dry, and dusty. Camels are the most common form of transportation in the desert.**

▼ **Kerala, one of India's most southerly states, is crisscrossed by inland waterways. It also has tropical, palm-fringed beaches.**

◀ *During the monsoon, many towns and cities are flooded. If the rains are particularly heavy, roads, railroad lines and fields may be completely submerged, and homes may be swept away. If the monsoon fails, however, crops are ruined, and people face hunger and drought.*

Because India is so huge, its climate varies considerably, with average temperatures ranging from 50°F to 86°F (10°C to 30°C). Snow falls in the north in winter, with temperatures falling below -3°F (-20°C), while summer temperatures in the far south can reach a scorching 114°F (45°C). There are similar differences in rainfall. The Thar Desert in the west has less than 10 inches (25 cm) of rain a year, while the Shillong Plateau in the northeast can receive an amazing 450 inches (1,140 cm) of rain a year.

The Indian climate is dominated by the arrival of the monsoon winds. The most important of these is the southwest monsoon. Its progress can be used to divide the year into three seasons — hot, wet, and cool. The hot season begins in February, when temperatures rise to over 103°F (40°C). Thunderstorms mark the arrival of the monsoon and the start of the wet season in June. The monsoon brings torrential rain, which is a welcome relief from the heat and vital for the success of

the farmers' crops. It comes to an end in October, when the cool season begins. This is the best time of the year in India. It is pleasantly warm without the intense heat and high humidity of the hot months.

In September or October the area around the Bay of Bengal, in eastern India, is often hit by violent tropical storms called cyclones. They cause terrible floods, which devastate the land leaving millions of people homeless.

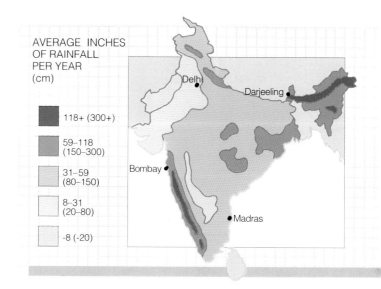

AVERAGE INCHES
OF RAINFALL
PER YEAR
(cm)

- 118+ (300+)
- 59–118 (150–300)
- 31–59 (80–150)
- 8–31 (20–80)
- -8 (-20)

KEY FACTS

● The monsoon brings about 70% of India's annual rainfall.
● From August 1860 to July 1861, about 1,042 inches (2,647 cm) of rain fell on the town of Cherrapunji in the Shillong Plateau.
● One million people were killed in 1970 when a cyclone hit the Bay of Bengal.

▶ *Goa, on the west coast of India, is famous for its tropical climate, its white, sandy beaches, and its warm ocean. These fishermen are hauling in their catch on Colva Beach in Goa.*

▲ *In the hot season, central India is unbearably warm, so some people retreat to the cooler hill country. During the* RAJ, *many British people spent the hot season in the hill town of Simla.*

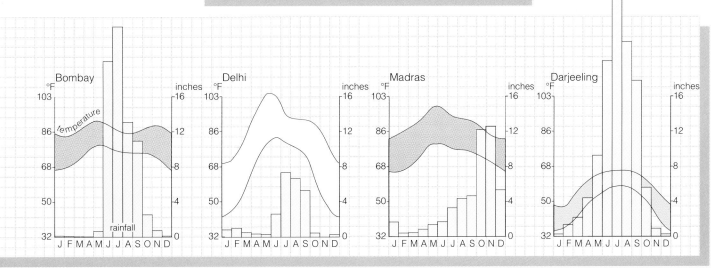

India's natural mineral resources include iron ore, bauxite (from which aluminum is extracted), and some copper ore. The country is one of the world's leading producers of iron ore. In 1990, it produced over 53 million tons of iron ore, from which it manufactured over 12 million tons of steel. Iron ore is found all over India, but some of the largest deposits occur in the states of Orissa and Bihar. A quarter of all mining in India is carried out in southern Bihar. Other natural resources include small amounts of gold, silver, and diamonds. Rajasthan is one of the principal areas where gemstones are found.

Much of India's energy comes from coal, which fuels the country's many factories. India has an estimated 120 billion tons of coal in reserve, enough to last it about 120 years. There are also huge reserves of petroleum, which have been found off the coast of Maharashtra and, more recently, in Gujarat.

About a third of India's electricity is generated by hydroelectric power. Half of this is produced by great snowfield reservoirs high up in the Himalayas. Huge dams have also been built across many of the major rivers to produce electricity and

▲*At this port, iron ore is being loaded for export. India's own steel industry also uses huge quantities of iron ore to make cars, motorcycles, bicycles, and so on.*

water for irrigation. In 1985, only about 2.3% of India's electricity was generated by nuclear power. This figure is expected to grow in the future.

Many Indian people, particularly in the villages, use wood or animal dung that has been dried in the sun as fuel for cooking and heat. The huge demand for firewood has put added pressure on the country's forests. Each year, 3.7 million acres (1.5 million ha) of forest are cut down to provide timber, paper pulp, and firewood.

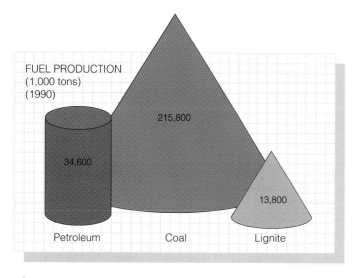

FUEL PRODUCTION
(1,000 tons)
(1990)

34,600	215,800	13,800
Petroleum	Coal	Lignite

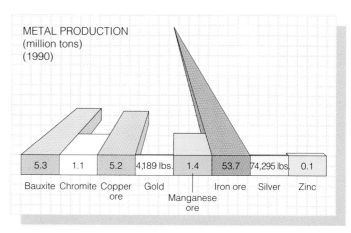

METAL PRODUCTION
(million tons)
(1990)

Bauxite	Chromite	Copper ore	Gold	Manganese ore	Iron ore	Silver	Zinc
5.3	1.1	5.2	4,189 lbs.	1.4	53.7	74,295 lbs.	0.1

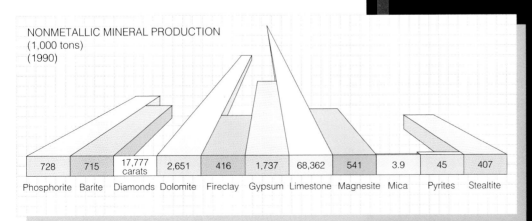

▲ *India is the world's third largest producer of cotton, after the United States and China. It is also the world's largest producer of jute, which is used to make ropes and sacks.*

NONMETALLIC MINERAL PRODUCTION
(1,000 tons)
(1990)

Phosphorite	Barite	Diamonds	Dolomite	Fireclay	Gypsum	Limestone	Magnesite	Mica	Pyrites	Stealtite
728	715	17,777 carats	2,651	416	1,737	68,362	541	3.9	45	407

KEY FACTS

● In 1990 India was the world's ninth major producer and consumer of primary energy.
● Animal and human power accounts for nearly 40% of all energy used in India.
● India produces over 11 million tons of salt a year.
● The 186.5 carat Koh-i-noor diamond, thought to have been found in Andhra Pradesh, became part of the British Crown Jewels in 1850.

GROWTH OF THE POPULATION

In 1991, India's population was about 844 million. It is the second most populous country in the world, next to China. The population has more than tripled since the beginning of the century and may pass 950 million by the year 2000. One in six of all the people on Earth live in India. About as many people live in the state of Uttar Pradesh as in all of Japan, the world's seventh most populous country.

Worried about the alarming growth of the population, the government set up a national family planning program as early as 1952. Each state has health centers and teams of nurses, midwives, and health visitors to advise people on how to limit the size of their families. This program has had some success, but on average, women are still having four or five children each.

There are various reasons for this. In India, the family is very important. Parents, children, grandparents, aunts, and uncles often live together under one roof. From an early age, children share their parents' workload. India has no pensions or benefits system, and parents rely on their children to look after them in their old age. Also, because about one in eight children die in their first year, parents often have more children to make sure some survive as adults. So better health care and financial support are also needed in order to persuade people to have fewer children.

VILLAGE LIFE

About 80% of Indians live in villages. There are estimated to be about 600,000 villages in the country, ranging from tiny hamlets to small towns. The villages often lack facilities such as clean running water, regular electricity, hospitals, or schools. However,

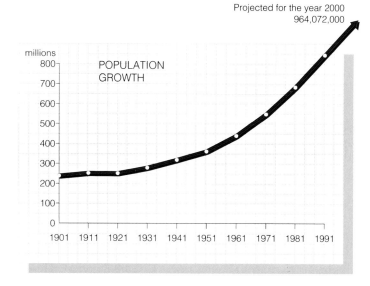

Projected for the year 2000
964,072,000

POPULATION GROWTH

there are many rural development programs to try to improve conditions. Village life often revolves around the well, where the women gather to draw water. Many villages also have their own temple or shrine. Most villagers earn their livelihood from farming. There are frequent village festivals, which celebrate sowing, plowing, and harvesting. Even if people move to the city to work, they may return to their villages for special festivals and celebrations.

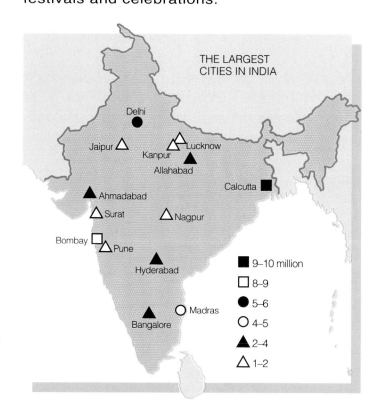

THE LARGEST CITIES IN INDIA

- ■ 9–10 million
- ☐ 8–9
- ● 5–6
- ○ 4–5
- ▲ 2–4
- △ 1–2

◀ *Village homes are usually simple and small. Some are built around a courtyard where the family cooks and eats.*

▼ *Calcutta is India's most crowded city. It has some of the worst poverty in India, but it is also a major center for industry.*

THE CITIES

The largest cities in India are Calcutta, Bombay, Delhi, and Madras. The city population is growing fast. The number of people living in Calcutta, for instance, increased from 4.6 million in 1951 to almost 10 million in 1991. This is partly due to the high birth rate and also because people are leaving the countryside in search of work. If they are lucky, they can earn nearly three times as much in the city as in their villages. Many find work in hotels, others as rickshaw drivers, peddlers, or domestic servants to wealthier Indians. Many of these workers live in unhealthy, cramped conditions in shantytowns or slums. Some live there permanently. Others might return to their villages once a year. In some cities, the authorities have tried and failed to tear down the slums. They are now trying to upgrade and modernize them.

POPULATION OF STATES (1981)		
STATES AND STATE CAPITALS		
53,549,673	Andhra Pradesh (Hyderabad)	
631,839	Arunachal Pradesh (Itanagar)	
19,896,843	Assam (Dispur)	
69,914,734	Bihar (Patna)	
1,000,000	Goa (Panaji)	
34,085,799	Gujarat (Gandhinagar)	
12,922,618	Haryana (Chandigarh)	
4,280,818	Himachal Pradesh (Simla)	
5,987,389	Jammu and Kashmir (Srinagar/Jammu)	
37,135,714	Karnataka (Bangalore)	
25,453,680	Kerala (Trivandrum)	
52,178,844	Madhya Pradesh (Bhopal)	
62,784,171	Maharashtra (Bombay-Mumbai)	
1,420,953	Manipur (Imphal)	
1,335,819	Meghalaya (Shillong)	
493,757	Mizoram (Aizawl)	
774,930	Nagaland (Kohima)	
26,370,271	Orissa (Bhubaneswar)	
16,788,915	Punjab (Chandigarh)	
34,261,862	Rajasthan (Jaipur)	
316,385	Sikkim (Gangtok)	
48,408,077	Tamil Nadu (Madras)	
2,053,058	Tripura (Agartala)	
110,862,013	Uttar Pradesh (Lucknow)	
54,580,647	West Bengal (Calcutta)	

UNION TERRITORIES
(islands and big city areas)

188,741	Andaman and Nicobar Is. (Port Blair)
451,610	Chandigarh
103,676	Dadra and Nagar Haveli (Silvassa)
51,602	Daman and Diu
6,220,406	Delhi
40,249	Lakshadweep Is. (Kavaratti)
604,471	Pondicherry Is.

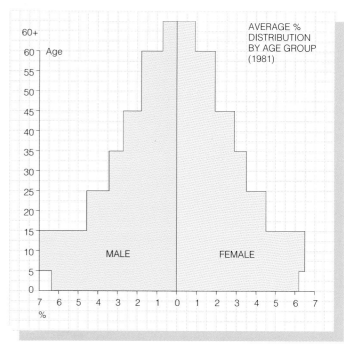

AVERAGE % DISTRIBUTION BY AGE GROUP (1981)

MALE FEMALE

▶ *These young girls come from Kashmir in the north of India. Kashmir is now a disputed territory, claimed by both India and Pakistan.*

INDIA'S DIFFERENT PEOPLES

People in India have different physical appearances, depending on where in the country they live. Those in the northwest tend to be taller and lighter-skinned than those farther south. People in the northeastern states tend to look more like their Chinese neighbors, with rounder faces and high cheekbones.

Tribal people, or ADIVASIS, make up about 7.5% of India's population. They belong to about 400 tribal groups and live mainly in the forests of east and central India. Millions of Adivasis have lost their traditional homes as the forests have been cleared for timber or to build mines, or have been flooded by hydroelectric dams and irrigation projects. Some Adivasis have now organized a protest movement to campaign for their own state, Jharkhand.

COUNTRIES WITH INDIAN COMMUNITIES NUMBERING OVER 40,000 (c.1980–84)*

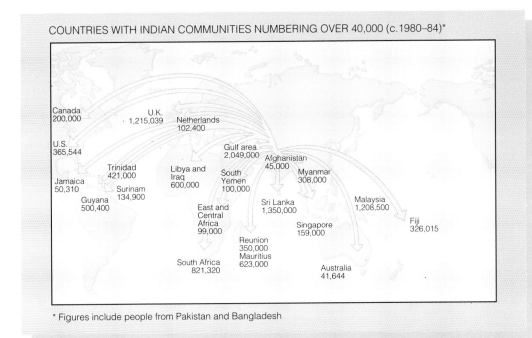

Canada
200,000

U.S.
365,544

U.K.
1,215,039

Netherlands
102,400

Gulf area
2,049,000

Afghanistan
45,000

Trinidad
421,000

Jamaica
50,310

Surinam
134,900

Guyana
500,400

Libya and
Iraq
600,000

South
Yemen
100,000

Myanmar
308,000

East and
Central
Africa
99,000

Sri Lanka
1,350,000

Malaysia
1,208,500

Singapore
159,000

Fiji
326,015

Reunion
350,000
Mauritius
623,000

South Africa
821,320

Australia
41,644

* Figures include people from Pakistan and Bangladesh

◀ *Since India's independence, many Indians have left India to live and work abroad. Many intended to return to India once they had saved up some money but never returned. This map shows the areas where there are now Indian communities of over 40,000 people.*

◀ *This woman comes from Gujarat, a state in the west of India. Many of the people of Indian descent who now live in the U.S. and the U.K. originally came from Gujarat.*

KEY FACTS

● A baby is born every 1.2 seconds in India. About 70,000 babies are born every day.

● In India, there is one doctor for every 2,520 people. (In the U.S. there is one doctor for every 370 people.)

● Most countries in the world have more women than men, but in India there are 93 women for every 100 men.

● The population of Delhi is expected to reach 10 million by the year 2000.

● About a fifth of city dwellers live in slums or shantytowns.

● Uttar Pradesh is India's most populous state, with over 110 million people. Bihar is second, with about 70 million inhabitants.

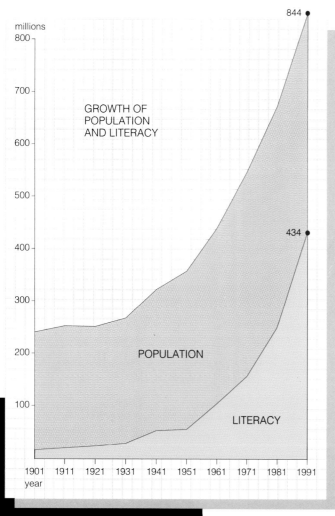

GROWTH OF
POPULATION
AND LITERACY

844

millions
800

700

600

500

434

400

300

POPULATION

200

100

LITERACY

1901 1911 1921 1931 1941 1951 1961 1971 1981 1991
year

When India became independent in 1947, it faced many serious problems. These included poverty, short life expectancy for its people, disease, famine, and little industry and commerce. It has come a long way since then, but many problems still remain. Despite its high level of industrialization, there is also great poverty in India. People still die of preventable

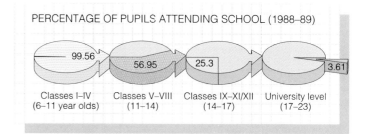

PERCENTAGE OF PUPILS ATTENDING SCHOOL (1988–89)

99.56	56.95	25.3	3.61
Classes I–IV (6–11 year olds)	Classes V–VIII (11–14)	Classes IX–XI/XII (14–17)	University level (17–23)

▼ **These children in a Delhi school are using slates to write on. Many cannot afford books.**

▶ **Muslim girls in this religious school study the Koran, the holy book of Islam.**

KEY FACTS

● India has one of the largest postal services in the world, with about 147,000 post offices.

● In 1968, there were only about 7,000 banks in all of India. By 1990, there were well over 50,000.

● More children work in India than in any other country, mostly in rural areas.

diseases, although great efforts are being made to improve health care. Western visitors often find it hard to adjust to the sight of beggars in Indian streets and to the hustle and bustle. But India is also a fascinating and welcoming place, with an ancient yet modern culture.

EDUCATION

India has a widespread, well-developed education system. There are state-run and private schools, universities, colleges and medical schools all over the country. The government provides free education for children between 6 and 14 years old, although some children drop out of school early or never go at all but work instead.

About 77 million Indian children attend primary schools, with another 40 million in secondary schools. In addition to formal schools and lessons, there is a system of "nonformal" education, where emphasis is placed on reading, writing, and practical health care or farming skills. Indian schoolchildren are expected to study hard. They are given plenty of homework, and there are regular exams.

Around 800,000 young people go to college or university in India. The country has 130 universities and more than 200 medical schools and nursing colleges. About 12,000 new doctors qualify each year and go on to work in government-funded hospitals or in private practice. India also

has an ancient system of traditional
medicine, called AYURVEDA. This system
uses natural herbs and oils, instead of
drugs, to treat illnesses.

FAMILY LIFE

Many Hindus in India live in traditional
extended families. Children, parents,
grandparents, aunts, uncles, and cousins
often all live together. The eldest man is
considered the head of the household, but
the whole family shares responsibility for
work and household tasks. Many wealthy
Indians employ cooks, cleaners, and nannies.

A wedding is an important and colorful
event in the family's life. Most Hindu
marriages are arranged by the couple's
families or by placing an advertisement in
the newspaper. In the past, the couple was
not allowed to meet until the wedding day
itself. They are now given time to get to

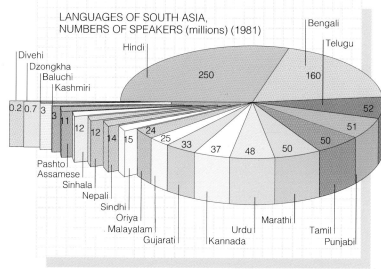

LANGUAGES OF SOUTH ASIA,
NUMBERS OF SPEAKERS (millions) (1981)

Bengali
Telugu
Hindi
Divehi
Dzongkha
Baluchi
Kashmiri
250
160
52
51
0.2 0.7 3
3
11
12
12
14
15
24
25
33
37
48
50
50
50
Pashto
Assamese
Sinhala
Nepali
Sindhi
Oriya
Malayalam
Gujarati
Kannada
Urdu
Marathi
Tamil
Punjabi

know each other and have the power to
refuse their parents' choice. To people in the
West, this system may seem rather cold and
restrictive, but many Indian marriages do
work well. After the wedding, a Hindu bride
leaves home and goes to live with her
husband's family. Traditionally, her parents

◀ *Homeless people are a common sight in India's biggest cities, such as here in Bombay. Unable to afford anywhere else to live, they sleep, wash, and cook on the street.*

▶ *A Hindu bride in her wedding finery. Brides wear special* SARIS, *often of red silk decorated with silver or gold thread, exquisite jewelry and makeup.*

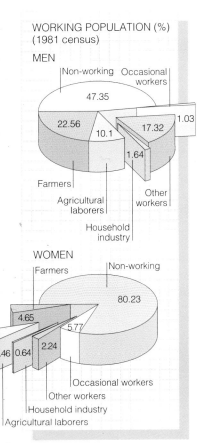

WORKING POPULATION (%)
(1981 census)

MEN

Non-working   Occasional workers

47.35

22.56   10.1   17.32   1.03

1.64

Farmers

Agricultural laborers

Other workers

Household industry

WOMEN

Farmers   Non-working

4.65   80.23

5.77

.46   0.64   2.24

Occasional workers
Other workers
Household industry
Agricultural laborers

▼ *Indians love cricket. Tickets to matches are highly prized, and the performance of the national team is followed and analyzed closely. Traditional Indian games include* KABBADI, *kite-flying, polo, and chess.*

KEY FACTS

● India has 15 official languages, including English, and hundreds of regional dialects.

● Hindi is the fifth most spoken language in the world.

● Over 27,000 newspapers and magazines are published in India each year.

● Seventy percent of people in Kerala can read and write but only 29% in Arunachal Pradesh.

have to send a dowry with her. This includes money, jewelry, clothes, and things for the house. There has been a great deal of criticism of the dowry system because of the tremendous financial pressure it puts on poor families.

RELIGION

Over 80% of Indians are Hindus. They believe in a supreme being, Brahman, who is represented by the three major gods — Brahma the creator, Vishnu the preserver, and Shiva the destroyer. There are hundreds of other gods and goddesses. Many Hindus worship in temples, considered the home of the gods on Earth. They perform PUJA, offering food, flowers, and prayers to the gods. Many Hindu homes have their own household shrines. Hindus believe in reincarnation (being reborn after you die). Their eventual goal is *moksha*, freedom from this cycle of rebirth. People who lead good lives move closer to *moksha* each time they are reborn. But Hinduism is much more a way of life than simply a religion. It covers

▲ *Hindu temples in south India, such as this one at Madurai, are famous for their elaborately carved gateways, or gopurams.*

▶ *The Jama Masjid in Delhi is India's largest mosque. Built in the 17th century by Mogul emperor Shah Jahan, it can hold over 25,000 people.*

FESTIVALS AND HOLIDAYS

The dates of many religious festivals and holidays vary from year to year.

January 26 REPUBLIC DAY
Celebrates India's establishment as a republic in 1950

February/March HOLI
Hindu festival to celebrate the beginning of spring

March/April MAYAVIR JAYANTI
The major Jain festival, marking the birth of Mahavira, the founder of the Jain religion

May/June BUDDHA PURNIMA
Celebration of the Buddha's birth and enlightenment

August RAKSHA BANDHAN
Hindu girls put bracelets, called *rakhis,* around their brothers' wrists to protect them from harm.

August/September JANMASTAMI
Birthday of Lord Krishna

September/October DUSSEHRA
Ten-day festival which celebrates Lord Rama's victory over the demon king, Ravana

October/November DIWALI, OR "FESTIVAL OF LIGHTS"
Marks Lord Rama's return from exile

November NANAK JAYANTI
Birthday of Guru Nanak, the founder of the Sikh religion

The most important Muslim festival is RAMADAN, when people fast from dawn to dusk for 30 days. Its dates vary widely.

every aspect of daily life and behavior. It also takes many forms. Some Hindus never go to the temple, others give up worldly goods and become holy men, or SADHUS.

Hindu society has traditionally been divided into four classes, or castes — the Brahmans (priests), Ksatriyas (soldiers and aristocrats), Vaisyas (traders), and Sudras (servants). Outside the caste system came the millions of "untouchables," who traditionally performed tasks that were considered unclean, such as sweeping streets. They were renamed Harijans (children of God) in the 1930s and are now known as "scheduled castes." Untouchability was officially abolished in 1950, but in some places discrimination still remains.

Over 11% of Indian people are Muslims, followers of Islam. There are also about 12 million Sikhs, 16 million Christians, 5 million Buddhists, and 3 million JAINS. The Buddhist and Jain religions were founded in India in about 500 B.C. In 1956, 3 million Harijans converted to Buddhism as a protest against the caste system.

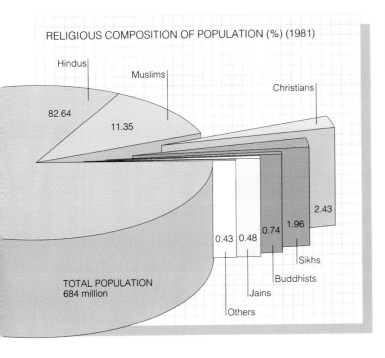

RELIGIOUS COMPOSITION OF POPULATION (%) (1981)

Hindus
82.64

Muslims
11.35

Christians
2.43

1.96 Sikhs

0.74 Buddhists

0.48 Jains

0.43 Others

TOTAL POPULATION
684 million

▲ *The Sikhs' holiest shrine is the Golden Temple in Amritsar. The Sikh religion was founded by Guru Nanak in the 15th century. Sikh temples are called* gurdwaras.

RULES AND LAWS

India became a republic in 1950. It is a union of 26 states and seven union territories (areas such as islands and large cities that are part of the union of India without being separate states). India is the world's biggest democracy, with a parliamentary system of government. There are two houses of parliament, the Lok Sabha (Council of the People) and the Rajya Sabha (Council of States). The president is head of state, and the prime minister is head of the government. Each of the states also has its own legislative assembly and chief minister. The national parliament is responsible for matters such as the courts, defense, overseas policy, and banking. The states manage their own police forces and schools. Special seats are reserved in the assemblies for tribal people and people from the scheduled castes.

▲ *The Indian government buildings stand at one end of an avenue, called Raj Path, in New Delhi. The parliament building is called "Sansad Bhavan."*

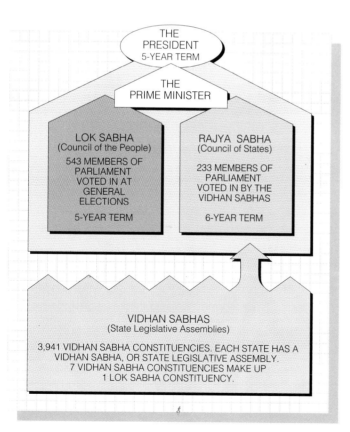

PRIME MINISTERS

Aug. 1947 – May 1964	Jawaharlal Nehru
May 1964 – June 1964	Gulzari Lal Nanda
June 1964 – Jan. 1966	Lal Bahadur Shastri
Jan. 1966	Gulzari Lal Nanda
Jan. 1966 – Mar. 1977	Indira Gandhi
Mar. 1977 – July 1979	Morarji R. Desai
July 1979 – Jan. 1980	Charan Singh
Jan. 1980 – Oct. 1984	Indira Gandhi
Oct. 1984 – Dec. 1989	Rajiv Gandhi
Dec. 1989 – Nov. 1990	Vishwanath Pratap Singh
Nov. 1990 – June 1991	Chandra Shekhar
June 1991 –	P.V. Narasimha Rao

◀ *Before an election, politicians tour the country. Huge crowds come to hear them speak.*

▲ *Republic Day on January 26 is marked in New Delhi by a military parade down Raj Path.*

All Indians over the age of 18 can vote in general elections. The main political parties are Congress, which has governed for most of the time since independence, and the Bharatiya Janata Party. The Communist Party is strong in West Bengal.

India fought a war with Pakistan in 1971, and the two countries are still in conflict over Kashmir. Indian troops and police have also been involved in the Punjab, where Sikhs are demanding their own state (Khalistan). In 1984, Prime Minister Indira Gandhi ordered the army into the Sikhs' holiest shrine, the Golden Temple in Amritsar. She was assassinated by her Sikh bodyguards in 1986. At the end of 1992, troops were called in to control rioting between Hindu and Muslim extremist groups in Ayodhya.

KEY FACTS

● In the Lok Sabha 78 seats are reserved for the scheduled castes and 41 seats for people from the tribal groups.

● Internationally, India is a key member of the NONALIGNED MOVEMENT, the Commonwealth, and the United Nations.

● According to new legislation, only people with two or less children will be eligible to become members of Parliament in the future.

● Over 1.5 million Indian people are members of the country's armed forces.

FOOD AND FARMING

More than two-thirds of people in India work on the land and depend on agriculture for their living. Most farms are only tiny patches of land, covering less than 2 acres (0.5 ha). Only a very few people own more than 25 acres (10 ha) of land. This patch of land has to provide food for a family to eat and sell. Families with no land of their own may work on other people's farms. They usually work for very little money. Many Indian states have a minimum wage for agricultural workers, but this is often ignored.

About three-quarters of the available farmland is used for growing crops. The main crops are rice and wheat, which form a large part of people's diets. Chick-peas, lentils, and beans are also important. Jute, cotton, sugarcane, and tea are grown largely for export. India is the world's largest producer of tea. Farmers also grow oilseeds, spices, groundnuts, tobacco, rubber, and coffee. Some cattle, goats, and sheep are kept for dairy products.

India's production of rice, wheat, and legumes has risen by an amazing 240% since independence, and the country is now self-sufficient in food. The 1988–89 harvest yielded a record 170 million tons of grain. The government keeps 20 million tons of grain in reserve, in case the harvests fail. The vast majority of farms depend on the monsoon rains for water. Only about a fifth get water from irrigation projects. If the monsoon fails, or heavy rains cause flooding, farmers can face hunger and ruin. So the government stocks of grain can help to prevent full-scale famine.

The so-called "Green Revolution" of the late 1960s helped to bring about improvements in India's agricultural performance. New varieties of rice and wheat were developed to give higher yields. Farming methods were modernized. However, it was the wealthier farmers who benefited most. Poor farmers could not afford the new seeds or equipment. Many still rely on traditional cattle or water buffalo plows to till their land.

Fishing is important along the coast, which is dotted with about 2,500 fishing villages. As with farming, traditional fishing boats (such as dugout canoes and catamarans) are still used alongside modern trawlers. About 3,189,000 tons of sea fish are caught each year. Fish are also caught in India's rivers, although river pollution has affected the catch in many places.

Like the people, language, and landscape, Indian food varies considerably from one place to another. It is also closely linked with religion. Mogul-style food is eaten in Kashmir, where a large percentage of the population is Muslim. Southern Indians are

GRAIN-GROWING AREAS

Wheat

Millet

Rice

▶ *Rice is planted in flooded paddy fields because it needs plenty of water to make it grow. These farmers are bringing in the rice harvest in Srinagar, Kashmir.*

▼ *About 1.5 billion pounds (720 million kg) of tea are picked in India each year. Assam and Darjeeling are famous for their tea. The picking is done by hand.*

KEY FACTS

● On average, Indians consume 2,204 calories a day, compared with 3,642 for Americans and 1,922 for people in Bangladesh.

● India ranks fourth in fertilizer consumption, next to the United States, Russia, and China.

● When famine struck Africa in 1985–86, India made the second largest donation of grain, next to the United States.

● Punjab is India's most fertile state. It is known as the "granary of India".

● There are about seven times as many traditional fishing vessels as mechanized fishing boats in India.

● Basmati rice is considered to be the best Indian rice. It is grown around Dehra Dun in the north.

● Bombay duck is a fish dish, not a duck!

▲ *These fishermen in Cochin, in southwest India, use Chinese-style nets to haul in their catch. Many different types of nets and fishing boats are used in India.*

mostly strict Hindus and strict vegetarians. Many Hindus are vegetarians, although some do eat fish and chicken. However, Hindus never eat beef, because cows are considered sacred animals. Muslims do not eat pork, which they believe to be unclean.

In Hindu households, rice or bread is eaten with almost every meal. More rice is eaten in the south, where it is widely grown. In the grain-growing north people eat many different varieties of bread, such as *chapattis* and *nans.*

Meals consist of several small dishes, together with pickles, *poppadums* (bread), and yogurt (*dahl*). Tandoori chicken is a very popular Mogul-style dish of north India.

The chicken is soaked in a yogurt and spice sauce, then cooked in a clay oven called a tandoor. The word *curry* is often used to describe Indian food, but there is really no such thing. It was a term used by the British to cover the whole range of spicy food they found in India. People eat from metal plates called *thalis* or from banana leaves. They eat with their right hands only. The left hand is considered unclean. Food is flavored with spices, such as chili, turmeric, coriander, and ginger. *Pan*, a mixture of betel nuts, lime paste, and spices wrapped in betel leaves, is often chewed after a meal to help the digestion.

Many Indian people have a sweet tooth. Most desserts are made of milk, rice, or nuts, but others include *kulfi*, a type of ice cream, and *rasgulla*, little balls of cream cheese flavored with rosewater. Sweet foods are often given as gifts and are specially made for weddings or other happy occasions.

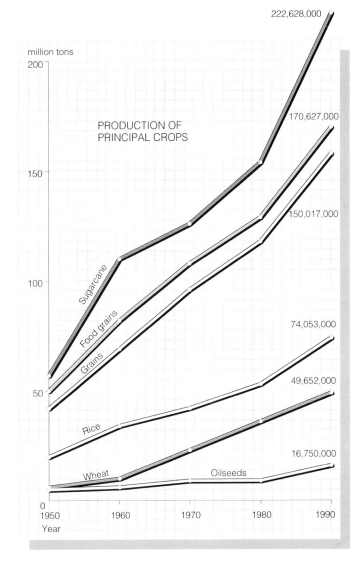

PRODUCTION OF PRINCIPAL CROPS

million tons

222,628,000
170,627,000
150,017,000
74,053,000
49,652,000
16,750,000

Sugarcane
Food grains
Grains
Rice
Wheat
Oilseeds

200
150
100
50
0

1950   1960   1970   1980   1990
Year

▲ *Cows are sacred animals for Hindus. They are never killed for meat. They are a common sight even in city streets, wandering among the traffic.*

▲ *Many farmers still use traditional cattle or water buffalo plows to prepare their fields for planting. They walk behind the plow, dropping seeds into the furrows.*

Since independence, India's industry has expanded rapidly, and it now ranks among the world's most industrialized countries.

India's major industries are based around its natural resources. Engineering plants make use of mineral reserves, such as iron ore and coal. Since the mid-1980s, production of electronic goods, especially television sets, radios, and computers, has expanded rapidly. Production of chemicals and petrochemicals has also increased. The textile industry, mainly concentrated in West Bengal, Tamil Nadu, Gujarat, and Bombay, is of prime importance. India ranks third in the world in the production of cotton goods, while jute is a leading export, too. Other major exports include engineering goods, leather, ready-made clothes, handicrafts, sugar, tea, and chemicals. Principal imports include fertilizers, petroleum products, iron and steel, pearls, and precious stones.

VILLAGE INDUSTRIES

About half of everything made by India's industries is produced by small, family-run businesses. Many cottage industries are based in the villages where traditional arts and crafts are made by craftspeople, using skills that have been passed down through many generations. Over 10 million people now work in these traditional industries.

TRADE AND AID

At independence, India's major trading partner was the United Kingdom. Today, it

▲Leather goods are a major export and include shoes, traditional sandals (chappals), and handbags. These are made in both city factories and villages.

▶Indian crafts include tie-dye and mirror-work cloth from Rajasthan and Gujarat, wood carvings, and paintings on silk or cotton.

▶India's small car industry used to make just two types of cars — the Hindustan Ambassador (right) and the Fiat 1100. A new, modern "mini-car" is now being planned.

MAJOR IMPORTS AND EXPORTS BY PERCENTAGES (1989–90) (Rs10 million)

IMPORTS
(total R354,118,800)

EXPORTS
(total R276,814,700)

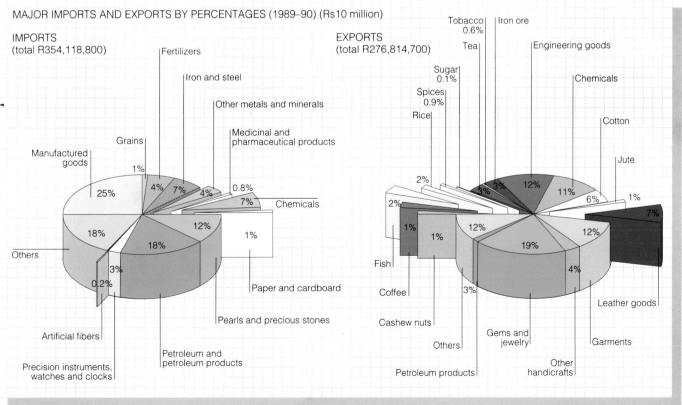

Imports labels:

Fertilizers

Iron and steel

Other metals and minerals

Medicinal and pharmaceutical products

Grains — 1%

Manufactured goods — 25%

4%
7%
4%
0.8%
7% — Chemicals
12%
1%
18%
18%

Others — 18%

3%
0.2%

Artificial fibers

Precision instruments, watches and clocks

Petroleum and petroleum products

Pearls and precious stones

Paper and cardboard

Exports labels:

Tobacco 0.6%   Iron ore

Tea

Sugar 0.1%

Spices 0.9%

Rice

Engineering goods

Chemicals

Cotton

Jute

2%
3%
3%
12%
11%
6%
1%
2%
1%
7%
1%
12%
12%
19%
4%
3%

Fish

Coffee

Cashew nuts

Others

Petroleum products

Gems and jewelry

Other handicrafts

Garments

Leather goods

The chart below shows the relative amounts of economic aid given to India by other countries.

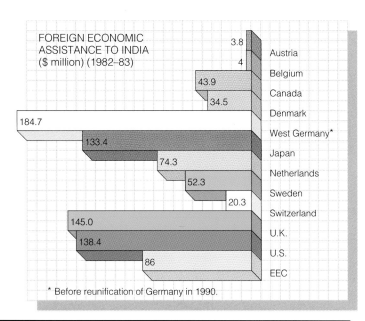

FOREIGN ECONOMIC ASSISTANCE TO INDIA ($ million) (1982–83)

Austria	3.8
Belgium	4
Canada	43.9
Denmark	34.5
West Germany*	184.7
Japan	133.4
Netherlands	74.3
Sweden	52.3
Switzerland	20.3
U.K.	145.0
U.S.	138.4
EEC	86

* Before reunification of Germany in 1990.

mainly trades with the United States, United Kingdom, Russia, Japan, Saudi Arabia, and Germany. It has some trade links with many other countries, but its overall share of world trade is quite small. India exports goods to 180 countries in total and imports goods from about 135 countries.

India's foreign debt has increased in the last 10 years because of its continued industrial expansion. It is now the third largest debtor in the developing world, next to Mexico and Brazil. In 1982–83, India received about $920 million in U.S. foreign economic aid. But India also gives aid to other Asian countries. Of this, Bhutan receives about 40%, Nepal 27%, and Bangladesh 18%. The rest is shared among 15 other countries.

MOVIES AND TOURISTS
India has an enormous movie industry, producing more movies than anywhere else

KEY FACTS

● India has the third biggest work force in the world (245 million in 1981), next to the United States and Russia.
● Forty percent of India's textiles are produced in the villages.
● In 1980, only 2 million Indians invested in the stock market. By 1989, this figure had risen to 10 million.
● About 9 million movie tickets are sold to Indian moviegoers every day.
● Shah Jahan had plans to build a black marble replica of the white marble Taj Mahal on the opposite bank of the Yamuna River .

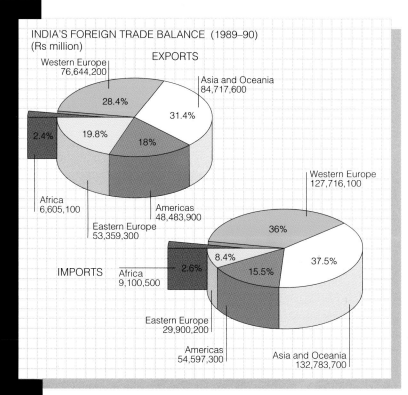

INDIA'S FOREIGN TRADE BALANCE (1989–90) (Rs million)

EXPORTS
Western Europe 76,644,200 — 28.4%
Asia and Oceania 84,717,600 — 31.4%
Africa 2.4%
Eastern Europe 19.8%
Americas 18%
Africa 6,605,100
Eastern Europe 53,359,300
Americas 48,483,900

IMPORTS
Western Europe 127,716,100 — 36%
Asia and Oceania 132,783,700 — 37.5%
Africa 9,100,500 — 2.6%
Eastern Europe 29,900,200 — 8.4%
Americas 54,597,300 — 15.5%

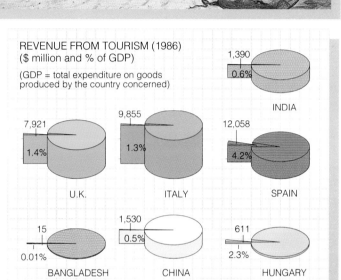

▶ *Filming takes place all over India.*
▼ *Huge billboards advertise the latest films. These brightly colored posters are often painted by hand.*

in the world, including the United States. More than 700 full-length feature films are made each year in India, mostly in Bombay, known as "Bollywood." Some are also produced in Madras and Calcutta. Indian films are usually action-packed with glamorous stars, songs, dancing, and romance. They are very popular. Going to the movies is a favorite pastime all over India. There are hundreds of movie theaters in all the major cities, while remote areas are visited by traveling movie vans.

Tourism is an increasingly important industry in India. In the 1960s, India was the favorite destination of hippies from the West. Today, luxury package tours take people to the Taj Mahal, the forts and palaces of Rajasthan, and the lakes and mountains of Kashmir.

▶ *It took 20,000 workers 21 years to build the Taj Mahal in Agra. It was completed in 1653 as a tomb for the wife of the Mogul emperor, Shah Jahan. He is buried next to her.*

REVENUE FROM TOURISM (1986)
($ million and % of GDP)

(GDP = total expenditure on goods produced by the country concerned)

INDIA 1,390 — 0.6%

U.K. 7,921 — 1.4%

ITALY 9,855 — 1.3%

SPAIN 12,058 — 4.2%

BANGLADESH 15 — 0.01%

CHINA 1,530 — 0.5%

HUNGARY 611 — 2.3%

◀ Buses can get so crowded that people cling to the sides and sit on the roof. Indian buses and trucks are often brightly painted and decorated with garlands of flowers.

	NUMBER OF CARS ON THE ROAD (1986)	
1,350,000	India	
19,929,000	U.K.	
22,000,000	Italy	
9,643,000	Spain	
50,000	Bangladesh	
250,000	China	
1,436,000	Hungary	

People in India seem to be constantly on the move — on their way to weddings or places of pilgrimage, returning to their villages, or going to visit relatives. The most popular form of transportation is the great railroad system that runs throughout India. The first stretch of railroad was opened in 1853, during the British raj. Today there are over 37,900 miles (61,000 km) of track, making this the largest railroad system in Asia and the fourth largest in the world. The journey time between Calcutta and Bombay, 1,024 miles (1,650 km), is 36 hours. There are several classes of travel on the train. The most luxurious is air-conditioned first-class. In 1987–88 the first stretch of subway opened in Calcutta, the first such system in the country.

India has four international airports: Palam (Delhi), Sahar (Bombay), Dum Dum (Calcutta), and Meenambakkam (Madras). Air-India is the international airline. There

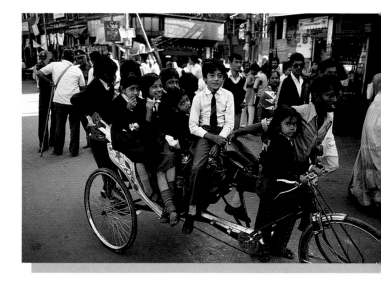

▲ These schoolchildren are crowded onto a bicycle rickshaw. Rickshaws may look precarious, but they are able to move easily in and out of traffic.

are 87 other airports for national flights on Indian Airlines. There is also a private national airline, called Vayur.

Bombay is India's largest port, handling a quarter of all shipping traffic. Other major ports include Calcutta and Madras. India has 160 minor ports, too.

There are now 535,376 miles (700,000 km) of surfaced road in India, but many villages are several miles away from the nearest road. Very few people can afford their own cars.

Other forms of transportation include rickshaws, which used to be mainly pulled by hand. Today, most are auto-rickshaws with motorcycle engines, or bicycle rickshaws. City streets are crowded with scooters, motorcycles, trucks, buses, taxis, and hundreds of people on bicycles. Calcutta also has a tram system. In the countryside people travel by camel, tonga (horse-drawn cart), and cattle-driven cart.

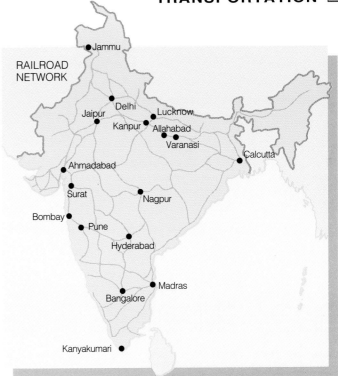

RAILROAD NETWORK

▼ *India's railroad system has about 11,000 locomotives, many of which are still powered by steam.*

KEY FACTS

● The longest road in India is National Route 7, stretching 1,474 miles (2,369 km) from Varanasi to Kanyakumari.

● In India, there are 12 cattle-driven carts to every car.

● The longest railroad journey is aboard the Himsagar Express, which travels 2,315 miles (3,726 km) from Kanyakumari in the south to Jammu in the north.

● The railroads carry 3.6 billion passengers and 60 percent of India's freight traffic each year.

THE ENVIRONMENT

apid industrial and agricultural development has done great damage to India's environment. For many of the country's poorest people, finding enough to eat and live on are more pressing problems than the state of the environment. But if the land is destroyed, their livelihoods will be destroyed, too. The government and conservation groups are now trying to implement policies to protect the environment.

Air pollution from power stations, factories, and cars is a major problem in many cities. The air in Calcutta, one of the world's most polluted cities, is often thick with carbon monoxide fumes from vehicles. In December 1984, one of the worst industrial accidents ever happened at the Union Carbide pesticide factory in Bhopal, Madhya Pradesh. Clouds of poisonous gas leaked from the factory and engulfed the nearby shantytowns. Over 3,000 people died, and some 2,500 are still suffering the aftereffects.

Few of India's cities and towns have proper sewage treatment facilities. Human and animal wastes are pumped straight into water, turning many rivers into open sewers. Many people still bathe and take

▼ ***Thousands of Hindu pilgrims travel to Varanasi each year to bathe in the sacred waters of the Ganges. Large areas of these waters are heavily polluted.***

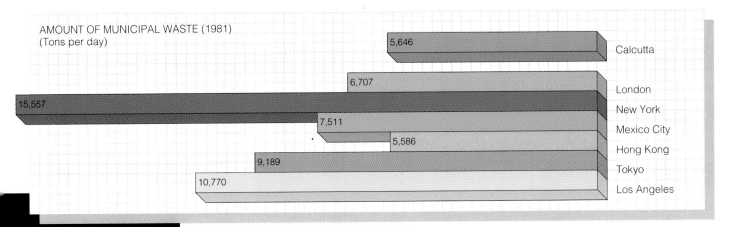

AMOUNT OF MUNICIPAL WASTE (1981)
(Tons per day)

	Tons per day	City
	5,646	Calcutta
	6,707	London
	15,557	New York
	7,511	Mexico City
	5,586	Hong Kong
	9,189	Tokyo
	10,770	Los Angeles

KEY FACTS

● About 70% of India's surface water is polluted.

● Three Indian children die from water-transmitted diseases every minute.

● About half of India's people do not have access to clean, safe drinking water.

● There are more than 300 wildlife and national parks in India.

● India has over 2,000 species of birds, including the peacock, which is the national bird.

▼ *Calcutta's garbage provides a living for thousands of people who sort and sell it. So many people live in the city's main garbage dump that a school was started there in 1981.*

drinking water from the rivers. As a result many suffer from water-transmitted diseases, such as cholera and typhoid.

About 372 miles (600 km) of the Ganges River are so polluted by human and animal waste, and by pesticides washed off the land, that the water there is dangerous to health. The Central Ganges Authority was set up in 1985 to tackle this problem. An action plan was drawn up, and $5.8 million was allocated to develop new sewage plants

along the river. The goal of the plan is to reduce pollution in the Ganges by 75%.

Soil erosion and deforestation are also cause for concern. Forests are being destroyed by mining and the building of dams. For example, the huge Narmada Dam project will provide water for irrigation and hydro-electricity. But it could flood 875,000 acres (350,000 ha) of forest and leave a million tribal people without a livelihood. Three-quarters of all the wood cut down in India is used as fuel. So much has disappeared that in some areas women spend most of the day collecting enough firewood to cook their family's meals. The problem does not stop there. When the trees are chopped down, their roots no longer bind the soil together. Heavy monsoon rains wash the soil into the

▲ Some of the major national parks in India. Animals, plants, and whole areas of the countryside, such as mountains and mangrove swamps, are protected.

◄ Most people in the countryside use firewood for fuel. Women in particular spend many hours collecting wood for their own use and sometimes for sale.

▲Over 300 species of birds, including storks and cranes, can be seen in the Bharatpur bird sanctuary in Rajasthan, which covers 19 square miles (50 sq km) of marshland.

◀Many maharajahs and British officers enjoyed tiger hunting. India had about 100,000 tigers in 1900 but less than 500 in 1970. Thanks to Project Tiger, an international conservation effort set up in 1972, tigers are now protected by law, and their numbers have risen.

rivers, which can become choked and, therefore, more likely to flood. Loss of this soil also leaves huge areas of land infertile. So the government has launched a massive reforestation program to plant 12.5 million acres (5 million ha) of trees a year.

Forest clearance and the needs of the growing population have also put much of India's wildlife under threat. National parks have been established all over the country to protect endangered animals, such as tigers and rhinos. Some parks and sanctuaries specialize in certain animals. The very rare Asian lion lives in the Gir National Park in Gujarat. Tigers live in Corbett National Park, Uttar Pradesh. Many parks were once the hunting grounds of maharajahs or British army officers.

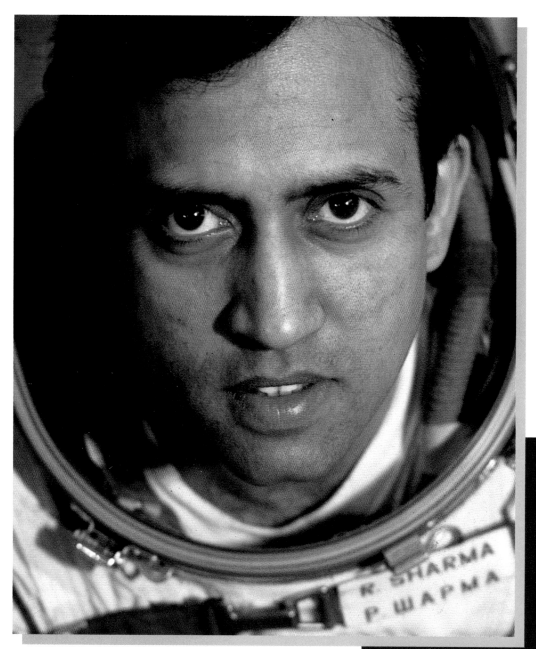 THE FUTURE

◀ *India's space program took a huge step forward when Rakesh Sharma became its first astronaut in 1984.*

▼ *The Indian satellite INSAT (Indian National Satellite) was launched in 1983 by the American space shuttle, Challenger. This communications satellite enables many remote areas in India to receive TV programs.*

India has achieved a lot since it became independent in 1947. It is changing and developing fast, yet its ancient culture is still very much alive. High-tech industries are now growing up alongside traditional ways of life.

India still faces many problems. It needs to find more effective ways of tackling poverty and pollution, and of improving health care. One of the most serious problems of recent years has been the violence between Hindus and Muslims. In 1990, riots broke out over a site in Ayodhya, considered sacred by both Hindus and Muslims. In December 1992, Hindu extremists attacked and destroyed the mosque which had stood on the site since the 16th century. In its place they set up a shrine to Lord Rama, whose birthplace they believe it to be. The Muslims retaliated with more violence, and hundreds of people were killed in cities all over India. There is a strong movement against such violence, as the vast majority of Indians wish their country to be a peaceful, tolerant, and united place.

Despite its problems, India has made many advances, especially in science and technology. It is one of the few countries to

have developed a nuclear bomb and to have sent satellites into orbit around the Earth. In 1984, Rakesh Sharma became the first Indian in space when he flew on board the Russian Soyuz T-11 spacecraft. One of his tasks was to perform yoga exercises in the weightless conditions, demonstrating again the mixture of old and new which makes up India.

▼ *Population growth is the greatest problem India will face in the 21st century. So family planning is vital.*

● AIR-INDIA
345 Park Avenue, New York, NY 10154
● CONSULATE GENERAL OF INDIA
3 E. 64th Street, New York, NY 10021
● EMBASSY OF INDIA
2107 Massachusetts Ave N.W.
Washington, D.C. 20008
● INDIA TOURIST OFFICE
30 Rockefeller Plaza North, New York, NY
10112

BOOKS ABOUT INDIA

Das, Prodeepta. *India.* Watts, 1990
Hussain, Shahrukh A. *India.* Trafalgar, 1992
Nugent, Nicholas. *India.* Raintree Steck-
  Vaughn, 1991
Srinivasan, Rodbika. *India.* Marshall
  Cavendish, 1991
Stewart, Gail B. *India.* Macmillan Child
  Group, 1992

GLOSSARY

ADIVASIS
The tribal people of India; they make up
about 7.5% of the population.

AYURVEDA
An ancient Indian system of natural
medicine

JAINS
Members of the religion of Jainism, founded
in India around 500 B.C. by Mahavira

KABBADI
The Indian sport of tag wrestling

MAHARAJAH
An Indian prince or aristocrat

MOGULS
The name of the Muslims of India who ruled
from 1527 to 1707

NONALIGNED MOVEMENT
A group of states, mostly from Asia and
Africa, not formally allied to either the
United States or Russia

PUJA
A form of religious worship for Hindus; often
a simple ceremony where prayers are said
and offerings of food and flowers are made
to the god or goddess

RAJ
The period of British rule in India, from the
early 19th century to 1947, when India
became an independent country

SADHU
A Hindu holy man

SARI
A dress consisting of cloth draped to form a
skirt and shoulder covering

INDEX

© Simon and Schuster
Young Books 1993

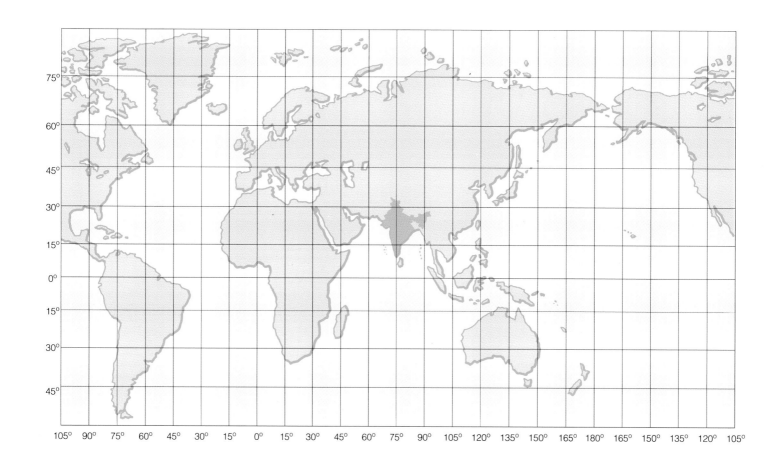